I'm Late!

AF450796

I Talk You Talk Press

CONTENTS

1. OH NO! WHAT CAN WE WEAR?

It was the last team practice before the big gymnastics competition in Burlingville. It was school vacation, but the high school gymnastics team had been training every day.

Usually, their teacher said, "You must do better! Try harder."

But today, she smiled a little. "Go home and rest. Remember, you must be here at the school at six o'clock tomorrow morning. Bring some snacks and water. The minibus will leave at six fifteen. Maybe this year we will be lucky, and win!"

Nerissa and Phoebe walked out of the gym together. There were five team members, and they were the oldest. This was the third time they had been to the competition. It was their last year at high school, so it was their last chance to win.

"Burlingville tomorrow!" said Phoebe. "It will take us a long time to get there. Last year we got second place. I hope we are luckier this year."

Nerissa laughed. "We have our wonderful new uniforms. I am sure we can win!"

Springtown High School was in the countryside. Most of the students' parents were farmers. It was not a rich school, but all the teachers and students worked very hard.

The gymnastics team made cookies and sold them at the market to get money to buy new uniforms. They were very pretty. They were blue and silver. Everyone in the team liked them very much.

Early next morning, the team and their teacher got on the minibus to start their long trip to the city.

"We will reach the railway station in Travers at about two o'clock," said their teacher. "Then we will take a train to Burlingville. We will be there by six o'clock. We must register for the competition by seven o'clock, so we will have plenty of time."

The bus driver took the bus through the country roads until they reached the motorway. Then suddenly, he parked the bus at the side of the road.

"I'm sorry!" he said. "There is something wrong with the engine. I must look."

Everyone sat in their seats and waited. They ate their snacks and drank their water. After about 20 minutes, the driver came back inside. "I'm sorry. I can't fix the engine. I will call my company and ask them to send another bus for you."

"Will it take a long time?" asked the teacher. "We must catch a train to Burlingville."

The bus driver looked worried. "I don't know. I hope there is a free minibus. I will ask them to hurry."

The teacher was very worried. She looked at her phone many times. Then she called the manager of the competition. When she finished talking, she looked very sad. She stood up and talked to the team. "I called the competition manager. I said 'our bus has broken down. Maybe we will be late.' But the rules are very strict. We must register by seven pm tonight. If we are late, we cannot join the competition tomorrow. We must try!"

It was 90 minutes before another minibus came. Everyone jumped onto the bus. "Please hurry," said the teacher.

When they finally arrived at Travers railway station, the teacher jumped out. "Please bring all the bags," she said. "I will see if there is another train. But I think it will be too late." Then she ran into the station.

The bus driver helped the team carry the bags into the station. They saw the teacher running back. She was smiling. She was waving tickets. "Quickly! Quickly! There is an express train! We must run."

Everyone ran as fast as they could. The bus driver was an older man, and he was a little slow.

There was just enough time to get on the train before it left. Phoebe fell into a seat and looked out of the window as the train left the station. She saw the bus driver running towards the train door.

"Oh, no!" she shouted. "The driver has our uniform bag!"

"Our uniforms!" shouted Nerissa. "Someone must get off at the next station and go back."

"It's impossible," said the teacher. "This is an express train. It will not stop until it gets to Burlingville."

They reached Burlingville at 6:45pm and ran to the big gymnasium. Luckily it was very near the station. They were just in time!

Everyone was very tired. It had been a long day. They were hungry too. There had been no time to get food at the station. They walked slowly to their small hotel.

"Come on everyone," said the teacher. "We must eat and then you must sleep."

"But what are we going to wear for the competition?" asked all the team. "We have no uniforms!"

"I don't know," said the teacher. "We were unlucky today. I will try to do something about the uniforms. Maybe the driver can bring the uniforms, but there is no train until tomorrow morning, and it will arrive after the competition starts." She looked very tired. Nerissa felt bad for her.

"Don't worry," said Nerissa. "Maybe something good will happen."

Nerissa and Phoebe sat in the coffee shop of the hotel. They ordered sandwiches and tea, but when the waiter brought their meals, they didn't feel like eating.

Then Phoebe said, "Oh no! Look who is at that table over there!"

Nerissa looked. It was the team from Maidstone High School. Maidstone High School was a rich private school. Their gymnastics team often won the competition.

One of the Maidstone team members saw them looking. She got up and walked over to their table. "Hi!" she said. "I remember you! You were here last year. You're from Springtown, aren't you?"

Nerissa and Phoebe didn't want to talk to her. They remembered her too. Her name was Maddy. She was very beautiful. She was a good gymnast. I don't want to talk to her, thought Nerissa. She is so proud!

"Cheer up!" said Maddy. "The competition is tomorrow. You know the judges like to see us smile."

Suddenly, Phoebe started to cry. "We won't be in the competition tomorrow. We lost our uniforms, and we have nothing to wear!" she shouted.

Maddy looked at them. "Stay here! Don't move!" she said.

She went back to the table where the Maidstone team was sitting. She sat down and started talking a lot.

"They are laughing at us," said Phoebe. "I hate them! Why are they so lucky and why are we so unlucky?"

Two Maidstone students ran out of the coffee shop. When they came back, they were carrying a bag. The five team members came over to Nerissa and Phoebe. They were all smiling.

Laughing at us, thought Phoebe and Nerissa.

Then Maddy said, "We have two uniforms. Tomorrow we planned to wear our blue and silver ones in the morning and our red and gold uniforms in the afternoon. Your school colour is blue, so we are going to lend your team our blue uniforms. We will wear red and gold all day."

Nerissa and Phoebe could not believe it. "You are so kind!" said Phoebe. "Why are you so kind?"

Maddy laughed. "You are a strong team. We want to win tomorrow, but if you don't join the competition, we won't know if we are really the best! Please take them."

"Thank you," said Nerissa. "We will try our best."

The other girls laughed. "Good luck for tomorrow! But not too much luck!"

2. TAKING THE TRAIN

Damian left his hotel and arrived at Hiroshima Station early. He was nervous. He had a Japanese exam at Hiroshima University. He had been studying for it for a whole year. He was from South Africa. He had been living in Japan for two years.

Which train goes to Hiroshima University? he thought.

He looked at the train map above the ticket machines, and found the station and fare. He bought a ticket.

I have my ticket, but I don't know which platform the train leaves from. Many foreigners will take this exam. My friend told me to get on the train with many foreigners. But I am very early. There are no other foreigners here yet, he thought. *I'll ask the man on the ticket gate.*

He walked over to the ticket gate and asked the man.

"Excuse me, which platform does the train to Hiroshima University leave from?" he asked.

"It leaves from platform five," said the man.

"OK, thank you," said Damian.

He went to platform five. There was already a train at the platform. There were some people on it.

This must be the train, he thought. *It will take fifty minutes, so I will have time to study before the exam.*

He got on the train and sat down. A few minutes later, the doors closed, and the train started to move.

Damian took his textbook out of his bag and started to study. The train stopped at every station on the way. More people got on, and some people got off. Damian looked at his watch. *Thirty minutes have passed. We will be there in twenty minutes,* he thought. He started to read his textbook again. Another thirty minutes passed. Damian looked up. *We should have been there by now. This is strange.* He looked out of the window. He could see rice fields and mountains.

This doesn't seem right, he thought. He looked at the woman opposite him. He walked over to her.

"Excuse me, I want to go to Hiroshima University. Do you know what time this train will arrive there?" he asked.

The woman shook her head. "This train doesn't go to Hiroshima University. It goes to Mihara."

"Mihara! But that's the next city!" said Damian. "I have an exam at Hiroshima University!"

The woman looked at him sadly. "You have taken the wrong train," she said.

The train stopped at a small station. Damian walked up to the driver's area and knocked on the window. The driver turned around and opened the door.

"Yes?" he said.

"I need to go to Hiroshima University," said Damian.

"This train goes to Mihara, not Hiroshima University," said the driver.

"What can I do?" asked Damian. He was so upset that he was nearly crying.

"Get off the train here, wait for another train which goes back to Hiroshima Station, and then take the right train from Hiroshima Station," said the driver.

"OK, thank you," said Damian. He got off the train and sat down on a bench. The train doors closed, and the train left.

Damian calculated the time. *If I go back to Hiroshima Station, I won't get to the university on time. I will be late. I don't believe this! I've studied so hard for this test for a year, and now I'm going to miss it. It's only held once a year. What am I going to do? I guess I could go sightseeing in Hiroshima. But I want to take my exam!*

A few minutes later, a train came. It was going to Hiroshima Station. Damian got on the train. He explained the situation to the conductor and bought a ticket. He felt sad as he watched the rice fields and mountains pass by. Then, he had an idea.

I don't know where I am, but I can try getting off at the next station. Maybe I can take a taxi.

He looked at his watch. The exam starts in an hour.

Ten minutes later, the train arrived at the next station. Damian got off and ran through the small ticket gate. He went out of the station and saw two taxis. He got in one of the taxis and said to the driver, "I need to go to Hiroshima University. I have an exam there in fifty minutes. Can you take me there?"

"Hiroshima University? That's far from here," said the driver. "It will take about an hour."

"Can you drive really fast? It is very important!" said Damian.

The driver looked at Damian. "OK, I'll try," said the driver. He drove out of the station and onto the road. Soon, they were on mountain roads.

Damian looked at his watch. "Faster! Drive faster!" he shouted. The driver drove faster.

There were many curves in the road and Damian and the driver moved from side to side. "Faster!" shouted Damian again.

After 35 minutes, the driver said, "Can you see those buildings over there? That's the university. We will be there in five minutes."

"Great!" said Damian. "I will be in time for my exam!"

The taxi drove into the university grounds. "How much is it?" asked Damian.

"Seven thousand yen," said the driver.

It is expensive, but my exam is more important than money, thought Damian. He paid the driver, said 'thank you', and hurried into the building.

"You are just in time," said a woman standing outside the exam room door. "Please find your seat and sit down."

Damian went into the exam room, and the woman closed the door.

Just in time! he thought. *Now I have to focus on my exam.*

Two months later, Damian got the results of his exam. He had passed!

I want to say 'thank you' to the taxi driver, he thought. *Thanks to him, I could get to the university. Now I have to study hard for the next exam level. And next time, I'm going to stay in a hotel near the university!*

3. BEVAN

Bevan was an artist. He was a very nice man. He was handsome, smart, kind and funny. Everyone liked him, but he also made everyone crazy.

He forgot things. He lost things. He never knew the time, so he was often late. People laughed. "You will be late for your own funeral," they said.

Bevan smiled and said, "I'm sorry. I must do better." But he never did.

When he married Marion, everyone said, "He will be better now. Marion is a strong woman. She will teach him to be on time, and not forget things."

It didn't work. Bevan loved Marion very much, and Marion loved her husband. This was good, because he made her crazy too. On their wedding day, he went to the wrong church. Then he lost his wedding ring.

Marion was not angry. She bought a new wedding ring. She showed it to Bevan and said, "This is your wedding ring. I am going to keep it for you." She put it in her jewellery box and Bevan forgot all about it.

They were happy together. Bevan was very romantic. When Marion asked him to buy eggs on his way home, he forgot to buy the eggs, but he bought some beautiful spring flowers for her. Or sometimes he bought chocolates or a silk scarf. He was always thinking of her.

One summer, Marion's sister was getting married. The wedding was going to be on a beautiful island. There was a five-star hotel on the island, and all the guests were going to stay there. Marion was very excited.

"It will be a very smart wedding. It will be very glamorous. I am going to buy a very special dress, and you will need a new suit!"

The Wednesday before the wedding, Marion went to stay with her sister on the island.

"I am going to help Philippa get ready for her wedding. You must catch the nine o'clock ferry to the island on Saturday morning," she said to Bevan. "Please don't forget."

Marion packed Bevan's bag with everything he needed for the wedding weekend. She put the bag next to the front door. She tied the ferry tickets to the handle of the bag. She put notes on the table and the refrigerator. The notes said --- *Saturday. Leave the house at 8:00am. Catch the 9:00am ferry. Don't forget. Don't be late.---*

When she was driving to her sister's apartment Marion thought, *I will start calling Bevan at six o'clock on Saturday morning. I will call him every hour. I will make sure he gets to the ferry on time.*

On Friday night, Bevan had an idea for a new painting. He painted for a few hours, and then he fell asleep on the sofa in his workroom.

He woke up at 8:00am. Marion had been calling him since 6:00am but Bevan didn't get the calls because he had forgotten to charge his phone.

Bevan went to the kitchen to get a drink. He saw the note on the refrigerator. He looked at the clock on the wall. *Oh no! I am going to be late!* He showered, shaved and dressed in jeans and running shoes. He ran to the door and picked up the bag.

The island is very beautiful, he thought. *Maybe I can make some drawings there.* He ran back to his workroom and took some pencils and a sketchbook. He opened the bag. It was full. *I need space. I must take something out.*

He threw some shoes and socks onto the floor, put his drawing materials in the bag, closed it and ran out of the house. He forgot to take his keys, and he forgot to lock the door.

He found a taxi and asked the driver to drive quickly to the ferry terminal. When the taxi arrived there, he saw the 9:00am ferry leaving. Bevan was too late!

Bevan thanked the taxi driver and paid him. He ran to the ticket office and asked about the next ferry.

"It will leave at twelve noon," said the ticket seller. "It will get to the island at two thirty pm."

That's too late! thought Bevan. *The wedding is at two o'clock. Marion will be so angry. Why am I so stupid?*

He walked away from the ticket office. He walked along the beach. He saw a small fishing boat on the water, and he had an idea.

"Hello!" he shouted. "Hello!"

The fisherman saw him. "Yes?" shouted the fisherman. "What do you want?"

"Can you take me to Tangaroa Island? I missed the ferry. I will be late for a wedding."

The fisherman didn't answer.

"Please!" shouted Bevan. "My wife will kill me if I don't get there. I can pay you!"

The fisherman laughed. "OK! But you will have to come out into the water. I can't come closer."

Bevan took off his shoes and socks. He walked into the water with his shoes and socks in one hand, and his bag in the other hand.

The fisherman helped Bevan climb into his boat. "What time is the wedding?" he asked.

"Two o'clock," said Bevan.

The fisherman looked at the sky and the water. He looked at his watch. "My boat is smaller and slower than the ferry. If we are lucky, we can get there by one thirty pm."

"Thank you," said Bevan.

It took a long time for the small fishing boat to get to Tangaroa Island. The fisherman and Bevan talked.

"What is your name?" asked the fisherman. "I think I've seen your photograph in the newspaper."

"My name is Bevan Petrie."

"Bevan Petrie? The famous artist? This is great! I don't want you to pay me. I will help you for no money. After the wedding, I want you to paint a picture of my children. Will you do that?"

Bevan looked at the fisherman. "I paint pictures of places. I don't paint pictures of people. But you have an interesting face. Do your children look like you?"

"One son and one daughter look like me. My other son looks like his mother."

"I will come to your house and paint a picture of your children," said Bevan.

The fisherman liked Bevan. He often looked at his watch. "I will take you very close to the hotel," he said. "But you must jump out of my boat. You must put on your clothes for the wedding and run very fast to the wedding chapel."

The fisherman came close to the beach. "Jump now! Hurry!"

Bevan jumped out of the boat. He went through the water to the beach. He was carrying his bag.

The fisherman looked down into the boat. "Hey!" he shouted. "You forgot your shoes!"

Marion was sitting in the wedding chapel. She was very angry. She was wearing her beautiful new dress. But next to her was an empty seat. *Where is Bevan?*

Everyone was waiting for the bride to walk into the chapel. Suddenly Bevan sat down next to her. "I am on time!" he whispered.

Marion looked at him. He looks so handsome in his new suit, and he came on time!

After the wedding, there were many photographs.

"Can Phillipa's family please come?" said the photographer.

Marion and Bevan joined the family group. Marion looked down. Bevan had no shoes or socks. "Where are your shoes?" she asked.

Bevan smiled. "My formal shoes are in our house and my running shoes are on a fishing boat."

4. A MISSED FLIGHT CONNECTION

Julian was from Traverse City in Michigan. He was on his way to New York for a job interview at a design company. He was in Chicago Airport. Things were not going well. He had missed his connecting flight. There had been a problem with the plane in Traverse City, and it was an hour late arriving in Chicago.

If I take the next flight to New York, I will be two hours late for my interview, he thought. *I should call the company and explain. I'm sure they will be fine about it.*

He found a seat in a quiet area and called the company. A woman answered.

"Hello, this is Julian Anderson. I have an interview at one o'clock," he said. "Can I speak to Ms Nelson?"

"Just a moment, please," said the woman.

A few seconds later, a woman said, "Hello. Tracey Nelson speaking."

"Oh, hi Ms Nelson. This is Julian Anderson. I'm calling about the interview at one o'clock. There was trouble with the plane in Traverse City, and I missed my connecting flight in Chicago. I'm going to be two hours late. Will that be OK?"

"No, it will not be OK," said Ms Nelson. "We are very busy here. I have other people to interview. I don't have time to wait for you. Let's cancel the interview."

"No, please," said Julian. "It's not my fault!"

"The interview is cancelled," said Ms Nelson. She put the phone down.

Julian looked at his phone for a few seconds. *I don't believe it,* he thought. *She was so rude! It isn't my fault that I'm going to be late.*

He went to a coffee shop and bought a coffee. *What am I going to do now?* he thought. *Should I go back to Traverse City? No, I can't do that. It will cost a lot of money to change my flight. I will go to New York. I have a reservation at a hotel for two nights. I will go shopping in New York and go to nice restaurants. I have never been to New York before. I am very disappointed about the job interview, but I will have a good time.*

Finally, Julian got on the plane to go to New York. He had a bag and a folder. In the folder, there were examples of his design work. He put his bag in the overhead locker and sat down with the folder. He didn't want to put the folder in the overhead locker. It was very important to him. All his best designs were in it.

Just then, a man in a suit stopped at Julian's seat.

"Excuse me, I'm in the window seat. Can I get past?" he asked.

"Sure," said Julian. He stood up and the man walked past him.

"Thank you," said the man.

The man sat down. He looked at Julian. "Do you work in New York?" he asked.

"No," said Julian. "I'm wearing a suit because I had a job interview. But it has been cancelled."

"Why has it been cancelled?" asked the man.

"There was a problem with the plane, and I missed my connecting flight in Chicago. I called the company in New York, but the woman cancelled my interview," said Julian.

"That's too bad," said the man. "What was the job?"

"Graphic designer," said Julian.

"Oh really?" the man was interested. "What was the name of the company?"

"Great Designs," said Julian.

The man looked at the folder in Julian's hands. "Are your designs in that folder?" he asked.

"Yes," said Julian.

"Can I see them?" asked the man.

"Sure," said Julian. He opened the folder and took out the designs. He passed them to the man.

The plane started to move, and soon they were in the air. The man spent a few minutes looking at the designs.

"These are really good," he said. "Great Designs has missed a great designer."

Julian smiled. "Thank you," he said.

The man took out his business card and gave it to Julian. Julian looked at it. He couldn't believe it. The business card said ---*'Philip Rowlands, Creative Director, US Design Company.'*---

Julian looked at the man. "You are Creative Director at US Design Company? That company is really famous!" he said.

The man smiled. "Yes, I am. And yes, it is a famous company. More famous than Great Designs. What are you going to do when you arrive in New York?"

"Check in to my hotel. Go shopping, go to a nice restaurant," said Julian.

"How about coming to my company for an interview?" asked Philip.

Julian looked at him. "Pardon?" he said.

"Come to my company for an interview. Your work is really good. I want the other directors to see it. Actually, we are looking for good designers to join our team. I think you will be a good employee for us," said Philip.

Julian was shocked, but he said, "I'd love to have an interview at your company. I'd love to show my work to the other directors."

"Great!" said Philip. "Come and see us after you check in to your hotel. The address is on my business card."

Later that day, Julian had his interview at US Design Company. Everyone loved his work. He got the job and moved to New York a month later.

Missing my connecting flight was a lucky event! he thought. *I'm working for a company which is more famous and better than Great Designs!*

5. IRWIN'S GRADUATION

The Freshest Bakery was in a small town called Balminster. It made bread for supermarkets in a nearby city. It was the only factory in Balminster, and almost everyone in the town worked there.

The bakery had been there for a long time and most of the machines were old. Sometimes they broke down, and they had to be repaired. The factory engineer was Frank. His job was to maintain the machines. He was very good at his job and most of the time there were no problems.

One Tuesday, Frank was finishing work. The manager came out of his office.

"You have a vacation day tomorrow," he said to Frank.

"Yes!" smiled Frank. "My son is graduating from university! He was the first person in my family to go to university, and tomorrow I will go to the graduation ceremony! I will leave home at six o'clock tomorrow morning. The ceremony is at the university at twelve o'clock. I will have enough time to drive there."

At 4:30am the next morning, Frank got a phone call from the factory.

"Frank! Frank! The big bread oven is broken. We can't make bread. Please come in and fix it."

Oh no! thought Frank. *I hope it is not a big problem. I hope I can fix it quickly. I'll take my suit with me to the factory, so I can drive from there to the university.*

When he arrived at the factory, all the workers and the manager were waiting for him. "Thank you, Frank," said the manager. "I know this is a big day for you, but we must bake the bread."

Frank got changed into his work clothes and went to look at the big bread oven. He could see the problem. He went back to the manager. "I can fix it, but it will take me maybe two hours. I will be too late for the graduation ceremony. I promised my son I would be there."

The manager felt very bad, but he said, "If we don't make bread today and get it to the supermarkets, we will lose our contract. Last time we had a problem, the supermarkets said, 'If you are late again, we will ask a bigger, newer bakery to make our bread.' If we lose the contract, we will have to close this bakery."

Frank looked at the workers. They were all his friends. There is no other work in this town. *If the bakery closes, everyone will lose their jobs. I must stay and fix the oven. I hope my son will understand.*

Frank worked hard to fix the bread oven. At 7:00am he finished, and the loaves of bread started rolling into the oven to be baked.

"We will be on time for our supermarket deliveries!" The manager was very happy. "You can go now," he said to Frank. "Enjoy your son's graduation."

"It's too late," said Frank sadly. "I cannot drive there in time. I have put a new part in the oven, so I'll stay here and fix the broken part. We might need it another time." He picked up his tools and the broken part and went quietly away to his workshop.

Every day when the bread was baked and packed and loaded onto the trucks, the workers had a break. They started work at 4:00am, so by 9:00am they were ready to eat and drink tea and coffee.

Usually they talked a lot and laughed, but today in the cafeteria, everyone was very quiet. Everyone felt very bad about Frank.

"Poor Frank," said Stan. "He is very proud of his son, and he wanted to go to the graduation very much."

"He stayed and fixed the oven so that we would not lose our jobs," said Victor. "I want to do something for him. Is there a way he could get there in time for the graduation?"

"Only if he had wings and could fly," answered Stan.

Glennis was sitting at the same table with Stan and Victor. She was stirring sugar into her coffee. "Fly..." she said slowly. "Fly..."

She took her phone from her pocket. "I have an idea!" She hurried outside. Victor and Stan could see her through the window. She was talking on the phone.

After about ten minutes she came back into the cafeteria. She was very excited. "Listen everyone!" she shouted. "Frank can go to the graduation! But we must all help, and we must hurry!

"My son, Wally, works for a helicopter company. I called him. I told him about Frank. His boss grew up in Balminster. He knows all about Freshest Bakery. He knows it is an important workplace in this town.

"If we can get Frank to the helicopter company in forty-five minutes, he will take him to the university by helicopter!"

"I'll go and tell him."

"Where is Frank's suit?"

"I'll drive him!"

"No, no! My motorbike will be quicker!"

Everyone was talking at once.

Fifteen minutes later, Frank was dressed in his suit. He was on the back of Victor's motorbike. Everyone came out of the factory and waved as the motorbike drove away.

At 11:40am, the students were standing outside the main university building. They were waiting to receive their degrees. There were many friends and family there to celebrate with them.

Irwin, Frank's son, was looking for his father.

He said, 'I will come', he thought. *I wonder where he is. I can't see him anywhere.*

Suddenly everyone heard a loud noise in the sky. They looked up. It was a helicopter.

The helicopter circled the university and landed on the sports field.

A man got out and started running towards the main building. When the man got closer, Irwin saw it was his father.

"I got here!" said Frank.

"Yes Dad, you got here. And I'm sure no one else's father came by helicopter!" said Irwin.

THANK YOU

Thank you for reading I'm Late! (Word count: 5,401) We hope you enjoyed the stories.

If you would like to read more graded readers, please visit our website http://www.italkyoutalk.com

Other Level 3 graded readers include
A Dangerous Weekend
A Holiday to Remember
Akiko and Amy Part 1
Akiko and Amy Part 2
Akiko and Amy Part 3
Be My Valentine
Different Seas
Enjoy Your Business Trip
Enjoy Your Homestay
I Need a Friend
Lincoln Takes a Trip
Match Day
Old Jack's Ghost Stories from England (1)
Old Jack's Ghost Stories from England (2)
Old Jack's Ghost Stories from Ireland
Old Jack's Ghost Stories from Japan
Old Jack's Ghost Stories from Scotland
Old Jack's Ghost Stories from Wales

Party Time!
Pretty and Bright
Stories for Christmas
Summer Days
The Curse
The Diary
Time to Go
Together Again
Who is Holly?

ABOUT THE AUTHOR

I Talk You Talk Press is an award-winning Japan-based publisher of language textbooks, graded readers and language learning/teaching resources. We won the Language Learner Literature Award in 2019 and 2020.

Our team is made up of highly experienced language teachers and translators, who have all studied at least one additional language to an advanced level.

This experience enables us to design our materials from the perspective of both the teacher and the learner. We consult with both teachers and language learners when designing our textbooks and graded readers, and test our materials extensively in the classroom before publication.

We are a fast-growing press, and currently publish graded readers for learners of English. We publish new graded readers monthly.

I'm Late!

www.ingramcontent.com/pod-product-compliance
Lightning Source LLC
LaVergne TN
LVHW051517170726
843492LV00002B/980